July 2020

DAILY YARNS

Maria Iliffe-Wood

For Ash,
without whom none of my writing would exist in the world.

Praise for Daily Yarns

"I found myself looking forward to Maria's daily posting of yarns. And I missed it when she stopped. The honest and straightforward words and expression of feelings felt personal to her and yet to me too."
   Coizie Bettinger - Artist

"I loved reading Maria's Daily Yarns. A myriad of emotions unleashed with 'what, you too!', to learning more about the author, being privileged to have that window open into her views, memories, feelings and emotions, all transcribed with such great penmanship."
   Maria Hanson MBE - CEO, me&dee Charity.

"I love Maria's daily yarns. I looked forward to reading them every day to see what showed up and flowed through her. Every day was different. It was fascinating to read the diversity of Maria's fabulous way with words!"
   Lucy Sheffield, artist and author of The Table without an Edge

"Maria touches the hearts of people with her writing. Her personality, her insight, gentleness, humour and observations on human nature are precise and honest. Each piece holds a wealth of wisdom, for the reader to observe, digest and savour. Certainly 5* Michelin food for thought."

Mandy Hunt - Psychotherapist.

"These daily yarns were a real treat to read every day during 'Lock Down'."

Jo Winchcombe

CONTENTS

Foreword

In March 2020, as COVID-19 spread around the world, my work dropped off a cliff and the effect of the pandemic became a reality in my life.

All of a sudden I had time on my hands.

In my inbox was a general request from a magazine for submissions of a piece of writing of less than 300 words called "Under Pressure". I decided to make a submission, which then sparked an idea that turned into a daily ritual of sharing short pieces on social media until the lockdown restrictions began to ease.

I shared my first post on 19th March and invited my friends and followers to offer two or three words which I would then write about and post. You will see, from the titles of some of the pieces, that they had great fun in offering me the most obscure of topics to write about.

Little did I know that what began as a bit of fun, would become the diary of a roller coaster ride, that was being shared by so many people. The yarns started off quite whimsical, but as we got further into the pandemic, what was happening in the world, and in my mind, started to show up in the writing. Though the yarns I explored the full range of emotions that I experienced from day to day, so the pieces range from reflective, to angry and frustrated, to sad and emotional, to calm and centred. If you take a close look, you may even find the occasional words of wisdom.

Every day it seemed that the pieces resonated with how people were feeling. I was not only writing about my experience, but the shared experience of so many people.

This is the entire collection of daily yarns, peppered with some of the pandemic milestones.

I hope you enjoy reading these as much as I enjoyed writing them.

Maria

DAILY YARNS

Diary of a Lockdown

Under Pressure

Last week I thought 'under pressure' meant tight deadlines, too much to do and not enough time. Back to back meetings, next steps, action points and moving forward with milestones towards almost impossible targets.

Time for friends squeezed into tiny gaps in my chockablock schedule. Time for family shoehorned into miniscule breaks between overrunning meetings, as the hands on the clock spun ever faster. Time for me... non-existent.

Today pressure is a yawning void, so much time and nothing to do. Work fallen off a cliff. No meetings, no deadlines, no goals. The kind of utopia I once prayed for.

Be careful what you wish for. It was a vacuum with no end in sight. The clock on the wall ticks, slow and languorous. Silence... yawns... between each tick

t i c k

t i c k

Time stretches out more than a sleepy cat on the sofa.

What is pressure anyway?

Niagara Falls thundering in my mind. A giant press

crushing the juice from my brain cells. Black tar oozing between the synapses in my head, and choking the life right out of me.

Why does it feel the same? The pressure of too much to do and the pressure of not enough to do?

Could it be that the pressure is all in my mind?

18th March 2020

Something's Happened

Something's happened, I don't know what, but it looks pretty serious. The whole world is shutting down but for what? I can't see it, feel it, taste it. I can't smell it. But I can see, feel, taste and smell the fear.

It's out of my hands. All I can do is stay at home, lock down, look after myself, and my loved ones… and the strangers who live next door, and the old couple that live across the road, and the disabled guy a few doors down, and my mum, who lives not ten minutes away, who I take for granted and don't see that often.

I can steer clear of people and smile at them from across the way, let them know they are not alone.

I can't hug or kiss my friends and family, but I can let them know I love them.

I can't work, all my clients have cancelled, but I can offer help and support through this wonderful thing called the internet.

I can self-isolate but stay connected to the whole world if I like, through the power of technology.

I can reach out to the world in love, compassion and kindness.

Something's happened to me. I find myself being kinder, being more considerate, more loving, more appreciative of my friends, my family, my husband, my home, my life.

And it's not only me.

Something's happened to others. I see others being kinder, more loving, connecting with others like never before.

Yes there's worry, there's fear, there's this virus that could devastate us, that's happened too. But something's happened in the world, and it may well be the saving of us.

19th March 2020

Portrait Philanthropist

I like to nod and wink at babies when I stand behind them in the queue at the supermarket. Their face lights up like Christmas and the games begin.

But you know what kids are like! They're like a dog with a bone and they can chew for hours. For me it's a long and winding desert road. I can only keep it up for so long!

I look around the store and focus on anything other than the electrified bundle on steroids in front of me. She thinks it's part of the game. Oh God why did I start this! It always turns out this way. Me all sweetness and light and within two minutes I'm a seething volcano. I resort to telepathic communication with the back of the mother's head. I mutely beseech her to save me from her little monster's vice like grip.

She's having none of it. She knows what's happening. She's concentrating on her shopping like an Exocet missile tuned into its target. There's no way she's going to draw the fire off me. How often does she get a moment's peace like this? When her little tarantula isn't throwing toys all over the place. Or opening the pasta and pouring it out. Or screaming for that bag of sweets she promised, that hasn't been paid for yet. Oh no! She's definitely not going to step in to save me. She knows these suckers don't come along very often.

And who am I to deny her a moment of peace?

So I paint on a smile, become the epitome of a portrait philanthropist, and offer this one small act of charity that gives a few moments of peace to a stressed out mum in the supermarket queue.

20th March 2020

Seasoned Suspecter

I suspect I won't know how this writing will turn out today. I'm doubtful about my own capability. I always think I won't be good enough, that everyone else will do better than me.

Write better.

Work better.

Care better.

Love better.

I harbor suspicions, I have doubts. I smell rats everywhere. Wherever I go, whatever I do, I'm waiting for the trap. I think it's just around the corner, ready to ensnare me, to bring me down and take me out.

One day someone's going to realise that I'm not as good as they think I am.

I already know that. It's old news. I'm a seasoned pro when it comes to knowing that I'm defective, under par, a second rate Sally.

So what if they suss me out?

Perhaps then I could relax. Perhaps then I could be myself. Perhaps then I won't have to pretend any more. Perhaps then I could stop. Stop being on edge, stop worrying what others think, stop suspecting all the time.

My name's Maria and I'm a seasoned suspecter and this is my tenth day dry!

God Took

It was the first day of Spring and I almost missed it. With all the furore in the world I forgot to notice. I usually watch Spring emerge, miracle by tiny miracle.

First, the twinkling, pristine, campana shaped snowbells.
    Then, the luscious, violaceous, smiling crocuses.
    Followed by the sunshine laughter of joyous daffodils.
    Then the pink snowfall of erubescent blossom.
    And last the high spirited, bouncing bundles of cotton wool lambs with curiosity filled eyes and soft pink noses that nuzzle in the fresh green grass.

This year I forgot to pay attention. Somewhere along the line of these frantic days, I stopped looking out for the signs.
    My focus was drawn elsewhere, to conversations about work, or, to be more precise, not working, and the frantic sorting out of quick fire changing plans. Hour by hour reviews and revisions of what to do next… or not do. Thinking and rethinking about who to talk to next. Trying to work out where I go from here… or not go, as self-isolation became the norm.
    I forgot to spot the sure-fire signs that Spring was on it's way, that warmer weather had arrived, that better times were

ahead, but it didn't matter.

God had it sorted it. God had it all under control and made sure that the flowers, the new life and the new season arrived just in time. God took care of it like God always does.

22nd March 2020

23rd March 2020

Boris Johnson announced the United Kingdom wide lockdown to contain the spread of the virus. People were advised to stay at home except for limited purposes, like shopping for essentials, one hour per day exercise and to travel to work only if it was absolutely necessary.

Dancing Salmon Trees

It's a beautiful morning. The sun is in a bright and shiny mood. The sky feels clear with no stains on its character. Its perfect blue is translucent and as I reach out to touch it, my finger slips right through.

The air is hushed as a quiet stillness has fallen over the earth. Life has a different quality to it today.

Love is riding the airwaves. I can feel its breath as it swims around houses, under cars and in through letter boxes. It holds and touches everyone with its cotton wool hands.

Kindness soars like a bird on a wing. It basks in the currents before throwing its warm, fluffy blanket and smiling face over the multitudes.

Compassion unfolds and unfurls its eternal arms and lavishes affection as it embraces and swathes the whole planet.

Blankety blank cheque book and pens hide at the back of the drawer, no need for these today. Sweet Alabamas ride roughshod over sharp nailed hot coals to simmer them down and blunt their edges. Dancing salmon trees sway in the cute winds of slowed down time and rest assured that picnics of socially distant relatives are balanced in mind and soul.

It's a beautiful morning. The sun is in a bright and shiny mood. And so am I.

Keep Healthy

I look after my mental wellbeing. In fact, that's about as good as it can get.

"But what about your physical health?" My brother, Tom said, when he came to visit a few weeks ago.

We were sitting in the lounge of my house. It was ten in the morning and I was still in my cream fleece dressing gown. My white Cross pen and hummingbird covered journal lay in my lap, as I was halfway through writing my daily journal when he'd arrived. The Missing Link, my favourite book by Sydney Banks, was on the table in front of me. I read a page every day and reflect on its true meaning. This is one of the ways I attend to my mental health.

It was obvious that I didn't pay attention to my physical health. I was two stones overweight. Tom was standing in front of me with his six pack, toned muscles and a furrowed caterpillar brow.

I'd eaten a Cadbury's crème egg the night before and I hoped that he hadn't spotted the foil wrapper scrunched into a small ball next to the book on the table. "Don't you worry about me." I said. And that was that. I never gave it a second thought.

But this Coronavirus is making me think again. Especially as I'm going to be at home all day, every day. If I keep going,

I'll be as big as a house in a few weeks. So now I am giving it some thought. I need to exercise. I need to eat well and in moderation. I need to do something not just think about it. It's not just about not getting the Coronavirus, it's about not becoming a couch potato. I know my mental wellbeing will survive but what about my body!! I need to look after that too.

24th March 2020

Brownies, Tea and Horseshoes

Sometimes, like today in fact! It's hard to write anything half decent. This is my fourth attempt. I tell ya! What's the story Jackanory? I need a kick up the Khyber Pass! Truth be told my writing has been brown bread in the water.

I write words on the page but Jeez Louise! My eyes are bleedin' with boredom. My fingers should be stretched on the rack. My pen should be ripped from its socket. The page should burn in hell.

So I've given up! I'm gonna write whatever rubbish or gibberish comes into my head. You know like;

Chocolate brownies ride queer street over haberdashered mosquitos. Or chameleon coloured squirrels take tea and biscuits with Chinese litterbugs and variant swastikas. Or even shiny horseshoes play candelabras with cheesy Wotsits over the counter of swinging see-saws.

It's gibberish! Who wants to read such tripe? What does it mean anyway? Does it mean something? Should it mean something? Maybe you can make meaning of it!

It beats the crap out of me!!

25th March 2020

26th March 2020

At 8pm, millions of people took part in a 'clap for carers' to show gratitude and appreciation for our frontline care workers. This would continue every week, and would grow to include appreciation for all essential workers.

Also Available

I was awake at two o'clock this morning. I was feeling my thinking about the Coronavirus and all that goes with it in this mad crazy current world. I'm sure I wasn't the only one who punched the pillow in an attempt to get comfortable. I'm sure I wasn't the only one, pulling my hair out and screaming at my head to shut up and go to sleep. I'm sure I wasn't the only one who hates, with a vengeance, being awake for hours on end, when all I want to do is sleep.

All I want is peace of mind. All I want is my thinking to stop. All I want is to live in cloud cuckoo land one hundred percent of the time. Wouldn't that be bliss? No worries, no stresses, no damned sleepless nights.

Why does my mind choose two in the morning to ramp up the volume and pick up the pace? Answers on a postcard please! I have no idea why that happens.

Lucky for me I have double vision. I can see all my worried thinking and know who I really am and know that the two are not one and the same. There is me and there are my thoughts. Who I really am watches the thoughts in my head, sees them for what they are and waits for them to pass by, without the need for me to do anything about them.

Don't get me wrong, I can still hate being awake for two hours in the night, but who I really am sees, watches and waits, for that too, will pass.

Underneath all the worry, the anxiety, the fear and the not sleeping, is peace of mind. That's also available. I may not always remember, when my thinking is going berserk, but whether I remember or not I know that it's true. It's not cloud cuckoo land, it's something much better!

26th March 2020

Mercury Points

I decided that I don't want to hate people, although arbitrary, querulous scrutiny can get in the way.

I decided that I don't like the feeling that comes when I find fault and put others down. I noticed that it's a double-edged sword and the steely sharp spike sticks itself right into my heart. It looks like the knife is aimed elsewhere, but that's just underhanded trickery.

Here's some other things I noticed; When I call someone a jerk, I feel like an idiot. When I shout at someone, I feel angry. When I judge someone, I feel the persecution. When I withhold love, I feel alone. When I ignore someone, I feel bereft. When I'm unkind, I feel shame.

I noticed that any thinking that I put out there, comes back at me like a boomerang Exocet missile with a perfect homing device and I experience whatever feeling I've just fired off into the ether.

Don't get me wrong, I'm not Little Miss perfect! I get hijacked by my thinking, but I have a secret weapon. Mercury points it out to me.

It's like I have an internal thermometer that measures the scale of my peace of mind. The mercury goes up and down based on my thinking and tells me whether I'm too hot, too cold or 'just right'. The mercury takes the form of my feeling.

My emotions tell me where I am on the gauge.

Here's what else I noticed; When I smile at someone, I feel happy. When I am kind to someone, I feel pleased. When I do something nice, I feel joy. When I see good in the world, I feel awe. When I give love to someone, I feel love. When I pay attention to what mercury points to, I can be in the 'just right' zone more of the time.

I decided that I want to feel love more of the time, and I noticed that the key to that is to give love. So I decided to give love to people and what d'ya know! I noticed that my world is a much happier place.

27th March 2020

Time on my Hands

Tick.   Tick.   Tick.

Tick.

I can hear the slow, studious deliberate clicks of the clock on the wall.

There is so much space between each mark of time. There's a lifetime in each soundless, suspended pause, it feels like.

Now those quiet interludes, those breaks of silence, those unfurling, scopious, stretches of emptiness have overtaken my calendar. Those neat packaged parcels of time are all empty.

Time yawns into the distance, as far as the eye can see. Weeks and months of it. It's too precious a gift to squander. I don't want to waste it on not urgent, not important, facile, trivial matters.

There are things I want to do, that feel important, yet somehow, I can't get motivated to start. I've got used to days with boxes of time allocated to this, that and the other. My time chockablock full with To Do List items, days when I would squeeze every last drop of juice from the gaps in my diary, knowing that time was scarce.

I don't want to be caught in that trap again.

Yet getting used to the new order, where space and time

are abundant is unsettling, uncomfortable, strangely discombobulating. The world has shifted on its axis and I need to regain my balance, to stay upright on this newly positioned planet.

I've got space in my schedule and time on my hands, which feels odd in itself, but what's even more strange, is the fact that I'm not worried about it. My mind matches my calendar, it's not so rammed with the usual stuff.

Worry? … No.

Anxiety?   No.

Fear?

No.

Where did they go?

Calm? Check!

Quiet?   Check!

Stillness?

Check…

Space?

Check…

Time to breathe?   Ah yes!

I have time on my hands.
Precious time.
A perfect gift of time.

28th March 2020

Fear Knocked

I get scared.

Fear is a deep ravine that I've teetered along the edge of, for my whole life. A constant undercurrent that threatens to pull me under and drown me. A ton weight yolk around my neck. It weighs me down, holds me back, tries to stop me from doing …….. well almost anything!

I heard a sharp knock on the door.

I was standing with one booted foot hovering over the precipice, the first step on a new journey. The abyss in front of me was dark and deep and wide. I carried a large rucksack filled with the heaviest stones I could find. Sweat poured down my face. I couldn't see for the salt stinging my sea green eyes.

There was something sinister on the other side of the door. I could sense the icy tentacles that waited to be allowed in, so it could choke the life right out of me.

Shadows of the Grim Reaper bounced around the room, trying to counter the heroic efforts of the summer sun, doing its best to light my way.

I had a vague sense of the path through my blurred vision. I had a vague notion in my heart that all would be ok. I had a vague sense that if I took the next step it would all work out.

I noticed a vibrant, soft pink, perfectly whole, untainted

rose petal by my foot, basking in an avenue of divine light along the side of the ravine.

"Who is it?" I said.

I opened the door. There was no one there. Fear had knocked on the door and I'd opened myself up to it, relying on that small glimmer of faith, deep within me, that knows that it's not real.

29th March 2020

Go On

Go on, it said, put one foot in front of the other.
    Go on, it said, you'll be ok.
    Go on, it said, there's nothing to fear.
    Go on, it said, I'll watch your back.

Go on, it said, I know it feels hard.
    Go on, it said, the fear isn't real.
    Go on, it said, it's all in your mind.

Go on, it said, climb that mountain in front of you.
    Go on, it said, you'll be glad that you did.
    Go on, it said, the view from the top will be worth all the
pain.

Go on, it said, I know your burden is heavy.
    Go on, it said, I will bear the strain.
    Go on, it said, there'll be joy tomorrow.
    But don't forget, you can find it today.

Go on, it said, do what feels right.
    Go on, it said, you'll do just fine.
    Go on, it said, you know that you want to.
    Go on, it said, I know that you can.

* * *

Go on, it said, the world needs this, it will feed mankind.

I know that you're scared. I know that you hurt. I know that
you grieve.
    I know that it's dark.

Go on, it said, there's light on the other side.
    Go on, it said, trust me.
    You know that I'm love.

Go on, it says, over and over and over again.

That sure steady voice that lives deep in my heart.

Go on, it said.
    I hear you. I said
    and I carried on.

30th March 2020

An Image Moment

Yesterday I watched a short video with David Attenborough throughout which he half spoke and half sang "It's a wonderful world".

Images flooded my mind. Not the images from the video, but images from when my dad died.

The phone call. The trip to the hospital. The nurse telling me the news, in the public toilet of all places! My mum screaming. The phone calls to my siblings. The Chapel of Rest. Registering his death. The arrival of a CD that I'd ordered a few days before, having no clue that his death was on the horizon. Listening to one of his favourite songs with tears pouring down my face.

I cried all over again, as the images evoked the emotion of those few days, twenty-one years ago. I listened to the beautiful words, that he'd lived his life by and I heard his message to me, both then and now.

The music came to an end and the tears turned to smiles, as I remembered all the love, the laughter and the fun times.

A lifetime of images came to me in that one short moment, relived and experienced like it was happening all over again. But images they were, recollections from the past, sad and happy, brought to me through the power of my memory.

I'm so grateful that I have that faculty. I'll take the bad with the good, if it means I can recall the special people in my life.

I stood in the kitchen and as that grievous period washed over me, it was coupled with gratitude for a man who meant so much to me. I'm so grateful that he is brought back to me again and again via images that appear in my mind at any moment.

31st March 2020

Pure Gold

I watch in blissful awe as beauty unfolds all around me, in the smallest acts of kindness, in the charity of millions, in the unselfish sacrifice of thousands of people at the frontline of this pandemic.

I see the photos of teams of people in science fiction uniforms, nurses and doctors praying in corridors, the grieving faces of parents separated from their children, sacrificing this precious time for the sake of the greater good, the faces of hospital staff after fourteen hours in ICU, blistered, exhausted, drained of every last ounce of energy.

I see delivery men, still delivering. Supermarket workers still stocking shelves. Pharmacists still doing their best under extreme pressure. Cleaners still cleaning. Water company workers still unblocking toilets. Construction workers still making sites safe. Care workers still caring. Suppliers still trying to supply. Neighbours helping neighbours. And so many more that I can't see from my safe, secure, locked down, home with my husband and daughter. Yet I know you are out there.

I see people sharing jokes and uplifting stories, funny video clips and serious advice to help others. I see people sharing the reality of what this virus can do. Thank goodness for those people that put out a warning to me and more like me, as yet untouched by the pandemic, so that I can see why I am asked to stay home and keep safe.

I see pure gold all around me. The pure gold of loving hearts, the pure gold of kindness and compassion, the pure gold of humanity.

1st April 2020

Walk Gently

I'm sitting here, steeped in anxiety, worrying about what the future might hold. I'm steeped in an underlying current of catastrophic and apocalyptic musings. I'm steeped in a dark black mulch that reeks of three-headed monsters that gnaw and prey and feed on my insecurity, my sensibility and my mental wellbeing.

I'm submerged in an ocean of such macerating magnitude, my credibility is sunk, my perky optimism is drowned, and the juice of my querulous, shape-shifting existence seems to be stemmed at the source.

I'm imbued with a vibe of preposterous machinations of kinetic insolvencies and retarded, back-stabbing generations of paucity.

I'm incredulous of never before seen facts, of situations never before thought possible, of stark realities that never before existed and nightmares that have reached never before heights of terror.

It feels like my existence has been usurped and my whole life placed in some parallel universe, in a science fiction movie of epic, fantastical proportions. It's like I'm swimming in a Salvador Dali painting when I'm more of a Monet fan.

I could get in a complete stew about these feelings yet I know to tread tenderly with these thoughts. I tiptoe my way around them trying not to block their way. I know that if I let them be, when they pass by on the other side, I will bathe in peace and calm.

Because I know that this will happen, it gives me comfort in these dark moments, for moments they are. I walk gently with my fears, aware that they are normal, natural and nothing to be afraid of. Life might be throwing me some curveballs right now, but with love and compassion in my heart I know that I am ok.

2nd April 2020

What Should 'Should' Do?

I should feel like I'm on holiday. But there's no holiday feeling in this head!

My heart feels locked in and shutdown. A hard crust has wrapped around the core of my existence. Like a Transformer, the armor plating rivets into place ready to shield me from any onslaught. It's too tight. In its protective custody I can hardly breathe.

I shouldn't feel this way. I shouldn't feel scared. I shouldn't withdraw. I shouldn't close myself off. I should know better.

All those 'shoulds'! Each one, a stab in my heart. All those 'shoulds' get through the gaps in this cast iron shield. All those 'shoulds' tighten the belt on this lead weighted straitjacket. All those 'shoulds' are traitors wreaking havoc from the inside out. All those 'shoulds', should shut the fuck up and leave me alone. That's what "should" should do!

I laugh at the absurdity of that. 'Should', judging 'should' and adding another layer of 'should' ballast to keep the chains anchored around my soul. As if they can in reality!

In reality my soul is unfettered. In reality I am always free. In reality I am a thinking human being that can scare the pants off myself through the power of my own thought. All those 'shoulds' are just made up rules. They can go to the hell where they try to take me. I refuse to go there anymore.

As I think this, I notice my heart loosens and my breath becomes easier. I feel a sense of calm.

There's still an undercurrent of fear but now I have room to maneuver. I have freedom to flex my wings, even if I'm not yet able to fly, and I have the space to kick all of those 'shoulds' right out of the park.

3rd April 2020

A One Piece Puzzle

Don't look at my shouting, my ranting, my raving, that's just me caught up in my thinking that there's something wrong.

Don't look at my depression, my worry, my angst, my hopelessness, that's just me losing sight of who I really am, beyond and below all the nasty stuff that goes on in my head.

Don't look at my sadness, my grief, my sense of loss, that's just me forgetting that I'm always connected to something greater.

Don't look at this body, with its grey hair, its wrinkles and its shabby exterior, that's just a cloak for who I really am inside this vehicle for humanity.

Look deeper, look inside, look beyond what I'm projecting. I'm in here, I promise you. Yes shrouded by fear and worry and anxiety, but I'm still here none the less.

I don't need to be fixed. I don't need to be put back together. I'm not made up of a million disjointed separate parts. I'm unbroken. I'm whole. I'm a one piece puzzle.

I forget that and that's why I sometimes behave the way I do. So please forgive me my human frailties and look beyond them to see the real me behind the screen.

4th April 2020

5th April 2020

Queen Elizabeth II made a televised broadcast to the nation. The fact that she did this was testament to the seriousness of the pandemic situation. She thanked people for following the social distance rules and paid tribute to all those involved in fighting the virus and keeping essential services going.

Boris Johnson was admitted to hospital after testing positive for Corona Virus. He was taken into intensive care the following day.

Terrible Twos

I'm staying home. I'm keeping myself and others safe. I'm holding it together or so it appears.

I'll tell you something for nothing! I want to throw myself on the carpet like a two year old. I want to bang my fists on the floor and thrash my legs in the air. I want to howl and squawk and scream at the top of my voice "IT'S NOT FAIR!"

Inside I feel wretched, scared, distressed at this querulous predicament I find myself in.

Stay home. Watch helpless as my business goes down the tubes. Gawp mutely as my income falls off a cliff. Stand by as my life disintegrates into a pile of shit. Don't go out. Protect others. While my entire existence goes to hell in a handbasket.

Don't get me wrong, I know why. But it doesn't make it any easier. I'm human for God sakes! Let me feel all this angst, let me be scared, let me bleat about how all this is so unfair, let me get it out of my system.

I know I'll only feel this way for a short while. It comes and goes. While I'm in it, it's real. When it passes, I see the illusion of it all.

I am like a two year old. I have a tantrum, then five minutes later, it's all forgotten. One minute I hate you, the next minute I love you. One minute, life is unfair, the next life is good. One minute the world is falling down around my ears, the next, it's a beautiful existence. I don't have any thinking about the fact that five minutes ago I felt distraught.

Watch out though! You know what those terrible twos are like! Any minute, I may have another outburst. Pay me no mind! Watch while it plays out. Bide your time. As sure as eggs is eggs, I will get over it and when I do, all will be well in the world.

5th April 2020

Toilet Rolls

"Is that a pack of toilet rolls?" I said. I was standing in the doorway of a shop that had been decorated to look like a Victorian grocery store. Before the pandemic the goods on sale were luxury items, local fresh foods and home baked loaves. The smell of sourdough bread lingered in the air and made my mouth water.

On the large oak table was an eclectic mix of standard groceries and exotic fare. Tins of baked beans sat beside dahl and Foie Gras. Organic chocolate and rosemary infused oil, alongside stock cubes and cornflakes. A sherbet lemon was on the floor by the table leg.

The big, round faced owner, who looked like he may have eaten just one too many of his home cooked pasties, was standing behind the table with his hands on his hips. He wore a faded brown apron, that looked like it came from an old box in the back of the shop, and on his hands a pair of blue latex gloves, both a sign of the times.

On the floor, by my left foot, was a brown paper bag filled to the brim with things off my shopping list. I was grateful to have bought pasta, tinned tomatoes and long grain rice. Things I'd not been able to get at the supermarket for love nor money.

The last time I'd seen toilet rolls for sale was two weeks

before. Our stock was running low and we'd already joked that we might have to use old newspaper, cut into small squares.

The owner grinned like the cat that got the cream and his green eyes twinkled.

"Yes." He said. "Who'd ever have thought I'd be selling them here."

Indeed! Who'd ever have thought that something so bog standard, (excuse the pun) would become something so special. Who'd ever have thought that life would change such that toilet paper would become a sought after treasure. Who'd ever have thought I would be filled with gratitude because I could buy a pack of toilet rolls. Yet grateful I was, and I wasn't going to miss my chance.

"I'll take some." I said. "Thank you very much."

6th April 2020

True Colours

OK – I'm just gonna lay it out there. When my writing isn't going well, it's because my ego has got involved – that's the truth of it. My ego thinks it knows better. What a joke ha!!

I can tell when it has shown up on the page. The writing gets boring, tedious, painful even. It's like pulling your own teeth out with a blunt instrument. Ego knows jack shit about writing but it's never let a lack of knowledge get in the way of an obdurate opinion.

I know from bitter experience that my ego can never write the kind of material that will blow a person's mind, or move a person to tears, or resonate with a reader's own story.

Yet it will throw its dummy out of the pram and sulk when it doesn't measure up to its own expectations and that shows up as disappointment, frustration or anger. Or it will put up one hell of a fight.

The thing is, ego knows it's not a patch on the Holy Spirit breathing through me, or the intelligence of life working its magic or God using me for its own unique purpose. Ego knows it can't compete but that doesn't stop it having a go.

Ego shows it's true colours day after day after day. It can't help but give itself away. It has its own identifying marks, its own unique pattern of spots, its own palpable texture. It's a dead giveaway, if you know the signs to look out for. My unique flavor of ego is judgement, criticism, expectation, feeling of failure, dejection and hopelessness, to name a few. It's true colours are black and white with no room for shades of grey, or any of the other tones on life's beautiful palette.

I can see ego's true colours and I tell you something for nothing, they're not beautiful to me!!

7th April 2020

Unicorns and Pots of Gold

I pictured my life as I wanted it to be. A perfect blend of coffee, magic roundabouts, unicorns frolicking and a chorus of angels that sang "It's a Wonderful Life", whilst they showered me with rainbows and pots of gold.

This is how I imagined my life could be, if only I worked hard enough. With the right amount of effort, why wouldn't my life be like that!

Then it became what my life *should* be like. My imaginings, my dreams, my childlike innocent hopes became a viscid, grueling quest, a checkmated juggling act aimed at prosperity, a gnawing, crucifying, impossible plucking expectation.

It became a massive stick, more like a cat o' nine tails, covered in sharp barbs, that I could flail myself with at every missed opportunity, every fatal mistake and every seeming failure of effort.

It became a fight, a battle, a day in day out concerted effort to do everything within my power to make it happen.

I was on a hiding to nothing. I'd been playing that game for too long and only just got wind of the fact that I was chasing an illusion, a fantasy, no escape to reality!

I didn't realise that's what I'd been doing, that my hopes and prayers had turned into expectation, that I'd started to measure myself against them and in doing so, made myself a failure, a no hoper, a big time loser. I hadn't intended to do that, but somewhere along the line I had those thoughts that seemed so real, I believed them and so the pursuit began.

Now I've seen it, I can stop chasing rainbows in the hope that I'll find that elusive pot of gold. I can give myself a break, relax and take it easy and see what life will bring me.

But hold on a sec, I think I just spotted a unicorn...

8th April 2020

Funny Old World

I hear the birds sing. I hear my neighbours talk. I hear the wind as it blows through the trees. Then I don't. They all disappeared for a moment. Then they came back.

It's a funny thing. This disappearance and reappearance. The world seems so real, but it doesn't exist in my mind for large chunks of time. Like the Coronavirus. It's all around, yet I forget about it for most of the day. What happens to it when I forget? Is it still there? Is it an illusion? Is it real? Is it all just part of one big dream that I have in my mind?

Some people say life is a mirage. But I can't buy into that idea… yet! I'm not saying that it's true or not true, I'm just saying I don't know.

If it's a mirage how come I can touch it, feel it, see it, hear it. Yet something doesn't add up that I'm curious about. When I'm asleep it seems like I fall into a different dimension. This world doesn't exist, yet another one seems to. Which is the real world? The one when I'm asleep, or the one when I wake up? Or is there another world, one that I can't touch, see, feel, taste or hear?

Sometimes I think I hear something from another dimension. Oh God! Does that sound like I'm losing my marbles! I hear in my heart and not my head and it feels like it comes from somewhere else, albeit it's inside me.

It seems like I flit between an external world, an internal world and another world. Is that true? I don't know the answer. I have so many questions and the more answers I get, the less I seem to know.

The one thing I know for sure though. It's a funny old world.

9th April 2020

Peace Warrior

I saw a rant on Facebook this morning.

It was a condemnation of the government's response to the pandemic. A vitriolic tirade, an invective harangue and a vituperous demand for more compassion in the world. It didn't feel compassionate to me.

My first thought was to respond in kind. To be sarcastic and ask 'where was his compassion?' I even started to type my retort.

Then I realised. Where was my compassion? My response was heavy with judgement, fuelled as it was by vexation. Was this what I wanted to put out into the world?

I stopped.

I could hear the clock tick, where before the sound had been drowned out by my peevish displeasure. My breathe slowed down and my heart rate settled as the noise in my head got quiet. Peace and love washed over me like a super soft silk sheet that embraced my soul.

I know what would have happened if I'd pressed "send". The diatribe would have continued, many others would have jumped on the bandwagon to bring their own version of hate and anger into the world. I didn't want to be part of that. I want to be part of the peace process not the hate process.

I pressed the delete button. No one saw my action. No one

is any the wiser. No one would have noticed, but I know that the world is a better place because I did nothing.

Today I was a peace warrior.

10th April 2020

11th April 2020

Queen Elizabeth II made another landmark speech, her first ever Easter address designed to rally the nation.

Later we would learn that on this date, the number of people in hospital with COVID-19 reached its peak.

On the 12th April, Boris Johnson was discharged from hospital and moved to Chequers to recuperate.

Easily Pleased

My body marks the passage of time. A wrinkle here and a whisker there. My skin, once smooth as a brand new silk sheet, now looks more like an unmade bed.

My body is getting weaker and my hair is grey. I grunt when I stand up. My joints creak and groan as they rail against my attempts to do the things that once upon a time I could do so easily.

I'm invisible in the street. No longer do I turn heads, receive wolf whistles or blatant looks of admiration.

My life is on a slow down. I'm unable to rush around from place to place. Tiredness washes over me when I try to do what I've always done. I feel the debilitating effects of a full diary that once I was able to take in my stride.

By now, I should have had a bigger house, a more luxurious car, more money in the bank and a pair of diamond earrings.

I thought I would hate it, but now that age is here, I find that I don't mind it at all.

Now I'm here I find that peace of mind is the greatest prize. I find that I have time to notice the little things. I find that I'm more grateful for what I do have. And I find that I don't need much.

I don't need the expensive gifts or the grand gestures. I'm

happy with a bar of chocolate and a nice cup of coffee. I'm happy with a good book to read. I'm happy with a bunch of daffodils on the hearth. I'm happy with a smile, a kiss or a hug.

I'm easily pleased these days and for that I am grateful.

11th April 2020

Corona Virus

I worry about the effect of Corona Virus.

I worry for the nurses, the doctors and all hospital staff on the frontline of the ravages of this disease. I worry for how they feel in the face of the loss of so many patients.

I worry for the people whose loved ones are ill and there is nothing they can do, not even visit. And for those who have lost family and friends and are unable to find comfort.

I worry for our leaders. I worry for how they cope with their own scrutiny, let alone the harsh questions of others, about their efforts to counter this virulent strain.

I worry for the journalists, the ones whose job it is to look for mistakes, who listen to the worries and concerns of the people, who people turn to when fear has overwhelmed them.

I worry for the postmen and women, the lorry drivers, the supermarket staff, the bin collectors and all those that we need to carry on working even thought it means putting themselves at risk.

I worry for the people who are doing their best to produce and deliver enough PPE, testing kits and ventilators. I worry for how they feel about not being able to deliver in time.

I worry for all those who have lost their jobs and for how that might play out in their mind.

I worry for those in lockdown, in unhappy or abusive relationships, or alone with their thinking.

I worry for all the people who worry about the Corona Virus, no matter what, or who or why.

I carry the worry for everyone, in the hope that it will lift a weight from their shoulders. I carry the worry, knowing its true nature and in the sure awareness that I can bear it. I help to carry the worry on behalf of the world, for this is what I can do in the fight with Corona Virus.

12th April 2020

Tangled Tail Chase

I hate getting into arguments. Not because I'm a coward, but because I can't think straight! I become a lily livered, blubbering idiot who can't string a sentence together. My mind goes into overdrive. It tangles up, turns itself inside out, back to front and upside down.

Candy lollipops twizzle around unchecked in the tornado. Jesus sandals whip themselves into a frenzy. Polka dot, tutu wearing hippos moonwalk in Japanese flip flops as my tongue cements itself to the roof of my mouth.

I have pigswill thrashing around in my head. I can't make head nor tail of any sensible contention and I'm dodging blades and arrows that are meant to hit their mark, but instead stab me in my own back.

Alphabet soup shoots out indiscriminate, unintelligible, addled impoundments. Joined up thinking no longer exists. Talk about freaking madness.

I get so frustrated with myself.

I want to be coherent, sound educated, be rational and calm in the face of my indignant, vexed displeasure, and then defend myself in a clear concise manner. Instead I can't even remember what I just said.

I wish I could make sense when I'm angry, but it just doesn't happen. Instead I have to wait for my mind to calm down, for the diatribe to settle and for a cool mountain breeze to blow the cobwebs away.

Only then do I see the wood for the trees. Only then do I realise that the thing I was up in arms about was something and nothing. Only then do I realise that my ego has got caught up in a tangled tail chase again. Poor thing!

My ego doesn't know that there's nothing to defend, that it only exists in my mind, a figment of my imagination. But by golly for something unreal it sure knows how to kick up a stink.

13th April 2020

Letting Go

I'm getting used to this staying at home lark. In fact, I'm beginning to love it. There's a part of me that hopes that it doesn't come to an end. It's given me an excuse to slow down and almost come to a full stop.

Things are changing and it feels new and fresh, not the same old, same old! I thought I loved the hustle and bustle. Turns out I'd just gotten used to it. It had become my normal and I see that there was comfort in its familiarity.

I'm realizing new things, noticing more, seeing what's important. It's not what I thought it was.

I feel different. I'm content with what's happening. I like the pressure being off and that there's no expectation to do anything.

I've been enjoying the things that cost nothing. Walks in the countryside with my husband, bike rides with my daughter, eating as a family, reading a good book, writing my daily yarns.

I'm taking one day at a time, doing what I like to do, not what I have to do. I like this feeling of freedom that has come from being locked down.

I'm letting go of trying so hard. When all this is over, I'm not going back to my old regime of self-induced pressure and expectation.

I'm letting go of the old me. I'm allowing her to rest in peace, grateful for what she did for me, loving that she cared so much and appreciative of her efforts to give me everything that I asked for, not realizing that what I really wanted was so much more simple.

I'm letting go of my old life and embracing a new one. I'm beginning again, starting over, with joy in my heart, love in my soul and gratitude for this opportunity to see a whole new way of being.

I'm letting go and letting God.

14th April 2020

Banged Up

I'm locked down twiddling my thumbs and it's only my just desserts. I placed all my eggs in one basket and now I ain't even got an omelette to show for it.

I thought I'd be riding high, instead I'm staring down these four walls.

Turns out I paid the wrong piper. I listened to the voice that led me down a dark alley and beat the crap out of me. I'd get back on my feet and dig in ready for the next round. I was gonna be top dog in this fight.

Right! You can see how that worked out. I squared up with that demon over and over. I wanted to prove that I was something other than dirt on its shoe, but I was on a hiding to nothing.

I didn't know I was in a boxing ring with myself. Round ten, ding ding, here we go again.

I may be pacing the floor, but I've stopped fighting with the voice in my head. On the outside it may look like I'm a failure, but I'm holding the top prize.

I've seen the truth of who I really am and it's not that whirling dervish of derision that lives in my head. It's the quiet voice of reason, the calm kind voice that tells me I'm ok, even when I don't think so, and no matter what I've done or not done.

I never knew that voice existed but I realise it's been there all along. I'm so glad that I can hear it now, otherwise I'd be going stark raving bonkers. I may be banged up, but I'm freer than I've ever been in my life.

15th April 2020

16th April 2020

The UK lockdown period was extended by another three weeks,
as the total number of people with COVID-19 surpassed 100,000.

Letting Go Part Two

Letting go and letting God – My ass! More like losing my grip on reality.

Yesterday I was in a cotton candy bubble of contemplative serenity and today I'm up to my neck in freaking quicksand.

I feel sick to my stomach with worry. I'm scrabbling around, desperate to earn a living but with no clue how to walk since I've been chopped off at the knees!

My mind is in a spin, a whirling dervish of procrastination, with shit hitting the fan and a bucketful of shoulds.

What the hell am I doing messing about, wasting my time writing these bleedin' daily yarns? I should be doing other things with my time – like earn a crust!

I know the money will run out soon and then what will I do!

I can't think straight. Nothing feels right. Whenever I think about what I should be doing, I feel querulous. There's something about that bandwagon that doesn't feel right.

The quagmire squeezes and chokes the breath out of my body. My arms are tied, bound and trussed like the legs of a chicken, behind my back in a straitjacket. My feet are weighted with lead boots, millstones drag me deeper into this oozing, bloodsucking, bog. My stomach is an agitated, churning cement mixer filled with boulders.

Where's my soft blanket of peace and calm? Where's my warm bath of gentle stillness? Where's the soothing balm of a mother's loving and tender kiss? Where's the hushed tones of my blissful quietude? I let it go, that's what I did. I lost my grip. Ask me what I'm letting go of today and I'll tell you, my bleeding sanity that's what!

Let go and let God? …. You're havin' a larf!

16th April 2020

True Worth

I look around at all the things around me and wonder why I have all this stuff. A vague memory springs to mind.

"You'll never amount to anything!" My mum said. She was spitting feathers. I was supposed to have finished my homework before she got home.

I was twelve years old, sitting at the dining room table, in my school uniform, with my thick red long hair hanging over my face. My life was an endless round of homework, chores and music practice. The upright piano smirked at me from behind mum's navy wool coat tails.

The smell of boiled cabbage and sausages hung around from the dinner I'd prepared for my siblings earlier.

The north facing window was locked down and shrouded by dark, heavy curtains that blocked most of the sunlight from entering the room. A tiny lightbulb did it's best to lift the mood, but with little success. The dimness of the room matched the weariness in my heart, tired from the pressure I was under to do well.

Toby, our Heinz 57, Labrador mix dog, looked sheepish in the corner, embarrassed by my red hair bobble attached to his ear.

"I wash my hands of you." She said as she turned on her heel.

I've been trying to prove myself ever since. All this stuff around me, I'd gathered over the years as evidence of my success. But it doesn't add up, because my true worth can't be measured in things.

My true worth is my existence. My true worth is who I really am. My true worth is not calculated by how much stuff I have.

My true worth is more precious than all of the things in the world put together and then some.

Why do I have all this stuff? The answer … doesn't matter. My true worth doesn't need to know.

17th April 2020

Love and Grief

Today is the anniversary of the day my brother-in-law died.

I can see the pain in my sister who still feels his loss so grievously. I can see the gaping wound caused by the loss of a man she loved, lived with and cared for, for over 30 years. I can see the impact of the hole in her life, the empty chair, the missing of the man she called her rock.

Today I am not able to be there with her, to tell her that she's OK.

There was a time when I thought that was my job, that it was up to me to ease her pain. But it's not. I see that now.

It's my job to be present, to hold her hand and stay with her while she navigates her way through this tumultuous storm. I know that she has an inner compass that will guide her home and it's my job to stay with her while she finds her way back.

I know that underneath all her suffering she is OK, and I know she knows that too, even if it doesn't look that way sometimes. Like today, when all she can see is the agony and excruciating heartache of her loss. But that's OK too.

She's designed to experience those things, as we all are. It's part of life.

Today I cannot hold her hand, but I am with her, in my heart, in my soul, in spirit we are together. She will hurt today and I will love her just as she loved him. I know that love will bring her back to her own OKness because love is always the answer. It's my job to love her and I will do that today and every day.

18th April 2020

Love You

I love you Mum.

Who would've thought it when for so long I thought you were Cruella da Ville?

I shut myself off from you, closed the doors of my heart and only ever came out to pick a fight.

I wanted you close and thought it was your fault that you weren't. I see now how I was to blame. How could you get close to this porcupine daughter, with poison in her quills, who would shoot them at you, whenever the whim struck.

I was a cow! I said horrible hurtful things to you. I thought you were the monster, when all along it was me. I was the demon, the back-stabbing minotaur who only wanted its pound of flesh.

I can't take back the awful castigations, the unjustified chastisements, the iniquitous, scalding tongue lashings. I wish I could.

I'm sorry I hurt you so much. I'm sorry it took me so long to see. So long to realise your love. So long to find out that I was a victim of my own thinking and blaming it all on you. I'm sorry I held onto the resentment for so many years. I'm sorry I kept us at arms length.

I can't say sorry enough. I have decades of bad behavior to make up for. Tell me how many Hail Mary's and Our Father's

I need to pray, to make up for the sin in my thinking, for my thoughts being so way off the mark, and I'll say them, for you, with gratitude and with love. Because I love you mum, more than you can imagine.

19th April 2020

Wild Goose Chase

I'm on a wild goose chase. I'm hunting down accolades, seeking compliments, wanting more likes, loves and comments on Facebook. Something tells me that these are real, that they're something to be desired, that they will make me feel good about myself, but all the time it's a stab in my back.

The more I get, the more I want, the more I need! It's become an addiction. I'm starving and the only thing that will sate my hunger is those damned emojis. But they don't feed me they just fuel the need.

20th April 2020

Who am I?

I am the I am that everyone seeks.

I am the I am that knows I exist.

I am the I am that sees the wholeness.

I am the I am that is universal.

I am the I am that constructs everything, even this sentence.

I am the I am that cannot be touched, cannot be tasted, cannot be smelled, cannot be seen.

I am the I am that observes, that sees, what these eyes cannot.

I am the I am with all the answers and none of them, because no answers are needed.

I am the I am that is the riddle of life.

I am the I am that cares less yet cares the most.

I am the I am that loves.

I am the I am that is and no more.

I am the I am that isn't what I think I am.

I am the I am that doesn't need an I or an am.

I am the I am that doesn't need to ask; 'Who am I?'

21st April 2020

Spread Love

What will I do today, from my lockdown home?

Maybe I'll spread wings and soar on a gentle breeze over hospital beds and shower the occupants with love. Then I'll move on to the nurses and doctors, the carers, the cleaners, the porters, the ambulance staff and every key worker, whether they are on the roads, in the supermarkets, on the streets or in the factories. I'll place my hand on their shoulder and remind them that they're ok, they're doing a good job and we love them so very much.

Maybe I'll fly like an albatross, over some journalists (not all mind!) and drop shit on them from a great height, a huge pile of stinking, festering manure, like the dung that they're trying to throw at our government and the experts who are doing their best to fight this invisible enemy. Or maybe I'll just whisper in their ear "There is another way you know, a kinder way."

Maybe I'll bring calm and blow inspiration into the minds of all those who are trying to solve the problems of this pandemic.

Maybe I'll sit a while with those who are alone, frightened and scared, those in abusive or unhappy relationships, those who are living hand to mouth, those who can't cope. I'll hold their hand and listen to their woes.

Maybe I'll go around the whole world and kiss every child who's doing their best to stay home and stay safe, with no clue what its really about. And not just the children, the parents too.

Maybe I'll say a big thank you to anyone and everyone for doing your best today, to put one foot in front of the other, even if it is only to pace the room.

Maybe what I'll do today is spread some love around.

22nd April 2020

Muted Voice

I thought I'd stopped paying attention to the voices in my head that told me how useless I was and how I had to prove my worth in ways that I'm not proud of.

I turned the volume down on one voice by turning up the sound on another. One that tells me I know something that others don't; I have the secret to life and it's up to me to share it with everyone I meet.

I muted one voice, only to hear another. This voice offers me Utopia if I would buy into its merchandise. It tells a good story, promises happy ever after. It sounds so different, so enticing, so seductive, it draws me in.

It took me a while to realise that I'd switched from hearing the ventriloquist, to listening to his dummy. It's the same voice with a different accent. The voice that sends me on a wild goose chase, forcing me into finding new and different ways to feel good about myself.

It pushes me to show people how good I am, but it's still the voice of that little child, that scared, fragile human being that is desperate to be liked.

I see that this new voice is like the Emperor's new clothes, another illusion, the same deception that I'd bought into before, just in a different guise.

I see how muting the voices in my head doesn't work, they

just find new ways to be heard. When I look them square in the face and see them for what they are, I can step back and away from them, into the calm space that surrounds them.

I don't need to mute the voices in my head, I just need to remember what they are in the moment – ego, my insecurities and anxieties just doing what they do.

23rd April 2020

Love and Loss

Twenty one years ago, I lost my Dad.

It was like a tsunami. It punched the air out of my lungs and knocked me sideways. It did its best to strike me down, drag me under and suck the life right out of me.

It blanched my life, took all the colour away and created a heavy dark fog in my mind.

A chain bound itself around my ankles, attached as it was to a ton weight. A heavy yoke pressed down on my shoulders. My wrists were cuffed and bound together.

My heart broke into a million tiny pieces and I carried them around, somehow aware that, in time, they would fuse back together again, albeit with a small piece missing.

I prayed for the pain to ease, knowing that no one could take it away from me. I knew that it was something I had to endure, that I would get through it, even though I had no idea how long it would take.

An endless well of tears poured from my eyes. Little did I know the healing in those tears.

Little did I know that even though he had gone, his love would remain as a cushion for my heart, a blanket for my shoulders, a light for my eyes to see, to follow until I got through the mist. Little did I know that he would hold my hand and walk with me until the storm had passed. Little did

I know that I would hear his voice over and over again, as he inspired and guided my actions.

His body departed this earth, but he never left me. He is in my heart forever. His love is always with me. As the deep, raw pain of his passing eased, it paved the way for beautiful memories that still make me smile.

I may not be able to see him, but I feel his presence every day.

24th April 2020

Fear

I pretend I'm not, but the truth is I'm scared. I don't know what the hell I'm scared of, you know all the usual stuff; rejection, failure, losing everything, getting egg on my face.

I know I'm scared because my heart beats extra loud, like it's going to burst right out of my chest. I hear a loud whoosh, like there's a storm in my ears. My hands are sweaty, and not just my hands. My legs are like jelly, like I've just done a hundred miles on a treadmill.

A boombox drowns out any ideas of the next step forward, it screams at me to stay where I am, not to move, it's too dangerous.

I hear every single voice that's ever said to me, 'you're no good', in Dolby HD Surround Sound, coming at me from every angle.

I don't know what to do for the best anymore. I don't want to put myself out there, I just want to hunker down, curl up into a tiny ball, stick my thumb in my mouth and hide in a corner where it's safe and no one can hurt me.

But there's another voice, a quiet calm assuring voice, that I sometimes almost miss, that says, 'go on, you can do it, you'll be ok'. And when I'm scared, that's the voice I listen to and I move on.

Love for Free

I always wanted the best things in life. I wanted special not ordinary.

I mean, why have bread when you can have cake?

Paste when you can have diamonds?

Hate when you can have love?

I go through life eating cake and what do I get? Bloated and fat!

I hankered after a pair of diamond earrings that I can't afford, but I'm no more or less happy without them.

I see now how special doesn't always mean good, nor does it give me what I think it will. I see that what looks like ordinary is often the most special of all.

I see how happy I am when I choose love over hate, kindness over selfishness, gratitude over desire.

Who'd have thought it could be so simple? That love is what makes all the difference. It doesn't cost anything and it doesn't have a negative effect. When the sages said 'Love makes the world go around', I had no idea what that meant. But now I've seen that there isn't a single problem that can't be solved from love.

Love for me. Love for you. Love for the planet. Love for what is. Love for free. (And we're not talking free love here, let's be clear about that!)

I'm here to give love away. Anyone who wants love, come here, I have some for you. I've got plenty.

Why give it away? Isn't that the six million dollar question!

Because it's endless and when I give it away for free, I get it back a hundredfold.

26th April 2020

27th April 2020

Boris Johnson made his first public statement after coming out of hospital.

Just two days before, the number of recorded deaths for COVID-19 had surpassed 20,000. The United Kingdom was the fifth country in the world to exceed this figure.

At the same time there was evidence that the lockdown was having a stabilising effect on the number of infections.

Plain Old Sadness

I sit in the chair and I don't want to move. A weight is holding me down. My arms are pinned to my side, my feet bolted to the floor. There's a fissure in my chest. A deep, wide gorge of an open wound, raw and open to the elements.

My body is too small to contain the scale of emotion that overwhelms my every cell. It overflows in the tears that fall from my eyes. I do my best to hold them back, but the endeavour is beyond my limited capability.

My heart keeps on ripping apart. Small things, little things, tiny things remind me and the pain surges over and over again.

It feels enormous, beyond colossal, the weight of the universe held in my inadequate hands.

It's the weight of love, boundless, unconditional, eternal love. Of course it feels heavy when I forget what it is. It's the stuff the universe is made of, that life is made of, that I am made of.

And it's plain old sadness too. All day, every day, common or garden feelings of loss and love combined. When I remember, I find that I can bear it a little easier, the load lightens and I can see it for what it is, that sadness is plain old love, pure and simple.

I'm Bored

I can't keep still. I'm a fidget bum as my old dad used to say. A memory springs to mind of when my mum used to make my primary school summer dresses.

"I'm bored!" I said. I was standing on a wooden dining chair, placed in the sunlight that streamed through the window, into the lounge of our small terraced house. I was wearing a pink gingham dress with an unfinished hem. It was the new uniform for spring term. We didn't have the money to buy an off the shelf dress so we went through this every year.

She knelt on the floor in front of me, with pins in her pursed mouth. Her short fingers held the bottom of the dress as she tried to pin it to at least some semblance of level!

My long, heavy, red hair tickled my face. I was dying to swipe it away but that would have really done me in!

My mum's hair, the same red as mine except it was short and curly, swam in front of me. The room spun like a top and all the colours melded into one. The piano, the table, the cupboards all raced into each other.

My slender legs and knobby knees felt flimsy. I swayed back and forth. The smell of sausages hung in the air and agitated the half eaten dinner in my stomach.

"Stand still!" my mum said sitting back on her heels.

"What's wrong with …" The next thing, I was aware of, was the ceiling. I was lying on the floor after having blacked out.

I didn't hear the end of the sentence, I didn't have to. I'd heard it so many times. There was something wrong with me because I couldn't stand still. I never mastered that art. I'm still a fidget bum. Maybe I'm missing the stay still gene or something! When I'm bored it reminds me of when I thought there was something wrong with me, but I stopped believing that a long time ago.

28th April 2020

Uncertain Goodbye

I said 'Goodbye' to you some weeks ago. I meant 'see you soon'. I meant 'stay safe'. I meant 'I love you'. I didn't expect that to be the last time I saw you.

I know we have other ways now of saying hello, how are you, I'm thinking of you, but I'm missing your smile, our hugs, our air kisses.

I miss hearing your laughter hit my eardrum, unadulterated by the large space between us. I miss the subtle nuances of your voice that get lost in the ether. I miss the vibes, the energy, the feeling that transmits, body to body, that underpin and underscore the love between us, that doesn't show up in the words, the banter or the mocking jokes. I miss holding your hand and feeling the love in that tenderest, most ordinary of gestures.

I worry about what I said to you last. I can't remember. I know we had our moments when we said things we didn't mean. Did you understand that it wasn't true, if I spoke in anger? Did you realise that I only ever meant to say I love you, no matter what the words spoken? Do you know that I can't wait to see you again?

This uncertain goodbye is a pain in the ass. Who knows when we'll see each other again, but in the meantime, just in case you don't know, just in case I haven't said it often enough, just in case this is the last goodbye, let me tell you right here, right now, in no uncertain terms.

I love you.

29th April 2020

About Daily Yarns

Forty-two days on the trot I've written a daily yarn. Every day I wonder if I will be able to write something. Every day I wonder if what I've written is any good. Every day I wonder if people will enjoy it. Every day I wonder if today is the day that no one will like it, that someone will discredit me and horror upon horrors, that everyone will ignore it and my words will lie dormant and neglected in the vast unseen algorithms of Facebook and Instagram. Indifference being the worst kind of feedback.

Every day I wonder if this is me finished, that the well of creativity has been exhausted, if that's me done. Goodbye, Sayonara, nothing more to be said.

Every day I'm astounded when something new and fresh has turned up on the page. Every day I'm relieved when I have something to show. Every day I breathe a sigh of relief, that today is not the day that I have to admit, to myself or my audience, that I'm dried up, washed up, bankrupt and trashed or that it's my time to be chucked onto the scrapheap of life.

Every day my ego jumps on the bandwagon and takes the credit, even though it knows that it played no part in this production.

Every day I switch from anxiety to pleasure, to gratitude,

to suspense, to fear and back again to gratitude, tinged with pride comes before a fall, just waiting for the crash and then getting back on the rails again.

It's a roller coaster ride, this daily yarn business. But lucky for me I like roller coasters!

30th April 2020

Peace

When I look into my mind, what is it that I see?

I close my eyes and see a kaleidoscope of light and shade and nuances of every colour imaginable, with no imagination making it happen.

When I close my eyes, when I look rather than listen, when the focus of my attention is on seeing rather than hearing… and my breathing slows down… and the noise in my head becomes the steady beat of my heart, the thump… thump… thump of the life sustaining engine in this miracle of a body, the reassuring backdrop to my existence… and my eyelids are closed curtains on the outside world, and I see white spots in amongst the colour… I feel a peace wash over me.

Peace like being in the embrace of a sheet made of the purest, softest silk. Peace like the quiet in the woods just before the dawn chorus. Peace like the joy of sunlight that sparkles on a millpond ocean.

When I look into my mind, what is it that I see?

I see peace.

1st May 2020

Gold Stars

I once strived for aspirational goals that had metamorphosed into impossible expectation. Working days that extended into nights, worried that I was going to fall short if I didn't send that email at midnight ready for the next morning's eight o'clock meeting.

It used to kill me. My spirit deadened, my energy sapped and my creativity destroyed. It pulled me down to the lowest common denominator of just getting by. Survival of the weakest my only instinct.

I'd put living my life on hold for career's sake. Life wasn't worth tuppence if I didn't have a good job to show for it. Everything got invested in the next promotion, the next high appraisal rating, the next big pay cheque.

All my eggs were in one basket. My worth dependent on one definition of success, those KPIs, those targets. My life reduced to five boxes on an annual piece of paper.

The glow would last for five minutes, then the shine would wear off and I'd be back to square one, chasing the next gold star.

I was driven by feeling not good enough and I believed that achievement would fix me. No matter how high the accolade, that feeling never changed. I was looking in the wrong place for the remedy.

Once I realised that I was already enough, I didn't stop achieving. No.

But I tell you, my life got a whole lot easier. My creativity blossomed, my productivity went through the roof and I found that I have time to live, as well as time to work.

I don't need the things I thought I did, like recognition, praise, top marks and high rewards. I don't miss the angst, the worry and the fear that goes with chasing my tail. I don't hanker after those decorations of distinction.

But that's not to say I don't enjoy them when I get them!

(Oh come on! I am human after all!!)

2nd May 2020

Scary Movie

I'm watching a movie called COVID-19 the Pandemic! It's full of scary moments, lots to fear and worry about, too much sadness, grief, pain and suffering and plenty to get angry and annoyed about. It's the full monty of human experience.

The thing, about this movie, is that I could be infected by something from the film. My body might catch the virus, my bank account might get depleted, my mind might lose its marbles.

All that being true, I know that the cinema screen is my inner world, responding to an outside world.

I see my thoughts, feelings and emotions ebb and flow in my body. It's a full body experience not just a bad head massage.

It amazes me that I can observe all this going on in my consciousness. I can watch this fantastical film and experience every nuance of feeling, from the safety of my chair. I can see myself go through every emotion, endure its full intensity and sometimes the excruciating pain of the feeling and yet know that I'm comfortable and secure in the movie theatre seat.

I don't like scary movies. I tend to choose kind and gentle films over ones that have a lot of anger and violence, but it seems like sometimes I don't have a choice. It's like there's another director in the projection room, who has the control panel and thinks it's funny to change the fabric of the film and try to catch me out.

It works. All of a sudden, I feel scared, or anxious, or worried, or angry and for a while I think I'm part of the movie.

Then at some point I remember I'm not the film, I'm the audience and I find myself back in my seat, feeling ok and watching events play out on the big screen of life.

3rd May 2020

God Crackpot

Yesterday my mum told me how my dad has guided her, since he passed away twenty years ago. There was a time when I would have scolded her for being so deluded.

In the same vein, I used to poohpooh Tarot readers and psychics, and people who saw angels. I thought they were charlatans who duped people out of their hard earned cash.

And anyone who mentioned the word "God". Boy did I ever have an aversion to that three letter word. If you'd have hinted that God was guiding me, you'd have felt the sharp edge of my tongue.

I'd have struck you off my list of trusted advisers. I'd have written you off as a crackpot. I'd have bundled you up with those shaven headed, purple robed types that wander around town chanting in some unintelligible language. I'd have put you down as one of those crazy old ladies, who hasn't showered for months and shrieks at everyone in the marketplace, that the end of the world is nigh.

Pope Francis said "God speaks to children in a way that they understand."

When I heard my mum yesterday, I saw that God has spoken to her in a way that she would listen.

God speaks to me through my invisible coach, a quiet voice that I don't always listen to, but talks my language. Those people I labelled as crazy, I now see as God speaking unique languages so that different people can be guided.

Now I'm one of those God Crackpots I used to despise! I talk about spirituality, true self and God. I do it because these Three Principles* have given me a new understanding of God and has brought me more peace than I ever thought possible.

If I'm not speaking your language, then I apologise. Don't pay me no mind.

4th May 2020

*Three Principles as introduced to the world by Sydney Banks - Go look him up!

Fifteen Minutes

I have fifteen minutes before I need to be somewhere else. What if this were the last fifteen minutes of my life?

I hope that I'd be calm, that I could enjoy these last few moments of life, and not take it for granted in the way that I have done before.

I hope that my last moments are filled with memories of love, that I don't have anything to regret in my life, that if I've hurt people, they already know that I am sorry.

I know that I will miss my family and friends because I love them so very much and I'd like to be satisfied that they know that.

I'd like to think that I would sit here in quiet, with Ash, and no words because the important thing has already been said, often enough for him to know, beyond any doubt, that I love him more than life itself.

I might contemplate what awaits me as I leave this body and maybe I'll be a little scared. You know, fear of the unknown and all that.

I hope that my faith that there is a great hereafter, filled with endless, unconditional love and spiritual essence will keep me strong. But truth be told if this is the end and there's nothing after this life, well so be it. Fat lot I can do about it anyway!

As I contemplate what the last fifteen minutes of my life might be like, I am filled with gratitude because now I know how I want to live the rest of my precious life.

5th May 2020

6th May 2020

The number of UK recorded deaths exceeded 30,000 today.

The top news stories all related to the government's difficulty in trying to fulfil the unprecedented demand for personal protective equipment (PPE) for the health service.

To Do List

I am a big To Do List fan. I like nothing better than to tick things off my comprehensive index of tasks to be completed. When I do extra jobs, I add them to the list, just so that I can cross them off! Every few days I rewrite it on a fresh sheet of paper, not forgetting to wrack my brain for all the other things that need to be added.

I love it when I can delete a lot of items in one go, so I do the quick jobs first but that means I leave the important things to last and then run out of time. What's that about!

I pray for the day when my To Do List is finished and I get the chance for a well earned rest. But that's an empty promise. The list is endless. It has a life of its own, like Jack's beanstalk that grew up to the sky, but this is real life right! You know as well as I do that the beanstalk could never reach its destination. The sky moves further away, the closer you get and my list keeps growing with it.

When I first started my To Do List, it was a useful tool, but now it's a double-edged sword.

"The road to hell is paved with good intentions." Ain't that the truth. I never saw my To Do List that way before. It was fuelled by good intentions but it became a huge stick to beat myself up with. Now if that's not the definition of hell I don't know what is.

Now I look at my To Do List in the same way I look at a hammer; it's a really useful tool for the job that it was designed for, like banging nails into a wall, but I'm not meant to hit myself over the head with it.

6th May 2020

Fifty Days

Fifty days since this pandemic became a reality.

Fifty days of social distance, of not meeting up with family and friends.

Fifty days of not knowing what the future holds and wondering how we'll cope.

Fifty days of horror stories in the news.

Fifty days of people putting their life on the line, day after day, just to do their job.

Fifty days of not being able to care for loved ones, and fear of death, of losing someone close.

Fifty days of daily beatings, of being locked down in a single room, not able to come out for air.

Fifty days of no money, no prospect of income, no food on the table.

Fifty days of relying on the goodwill of others, foodbanks, delivery agents and first responders.

Fifty days of wanting things to be different, of grieving for a lost world.

Fifty days of wondering why and how did this happen and who should we blame.

Fifty days of staying home as a family, of sitting around the table and eating home cooked food.

Fifty days of slowing down, less work and more exercise

and more cake than is healthy.

Fifty days of being grateful, of appreciation for what I once took for granted.

Fifty days of volunteering our time and services, of small acts of kindness and smiling at strangers, knowing we're all in this together.

Fifty days of love for our neighbours.

Fifty days of seeing life in a different way, of seeing what's possible.

Fifty days of optimism for a new normal and a better world.

Fifty days of separate realities, so many different experiences of the same pandemic.

Fifty days of writing this daily yarn, in the hope that it will bring joy to people's lives and perhaps an insight, that could change your whole experience of this curious world.

7th May 2020

Mood Match

My mood doesn't match the day.

The sun is so bright I need my sunglasses. The sky is one of those perfect cloudless, cerulean blue expanses of vastness. Everything is in sharp focus. I can see every blade of lush green grass and every red brick in the house across the road. Every leaf on every tree stands out against the brilliant backdrop. Even the shadows are more pronounced. I can see into every nook of the dark places, that would normally be hidden from the radiance of day.

Contrast that with the heavy funk. Shades of grey and charcoal. Black storm clouds, ear splitting thunderclaps, shrieks of lightning strike the earth and the noise fills my head and drowns out any kind of sense. Hailstones, golf ball sized blocks of ice, leave a dent in my equilibrium. The ocean's a tsunami, it swamps, gorges and devours everything in its path, leaving a chaotic destruction in its wake. It's on the scale of a worldwide disaster, screeching pandemic sized mood swings. The dense clouds hang so low, so close to the ground, they create blind spots and cover treacherous pitch-black holes filled with who knows what. I can't see my hand in front of my face.

It's so stormy out there. I'm so glad my mood doesn't match the day.

Human Design

I put myself out there, in clear view, in danger of being shot down. I make myself vulnerable to attack, to derogatory, sharp tongued judges with denunciations that are designed to castigate, chagrin and put me in a dark corner where children should be seen and not heard.

I was told that to be silent was golden and my opinion didn't count, but I retaliated. I wasn't prepared to live a quiet life. I was no shrinking violet. I wasn't designed that way.

I was designed to be quiet sometimes, but not to retreat back from action because of fear. I was designed to be angry so that I could counter injustices. I was designed to be worried and concerned and to care with a passion, so that I could make a difference in the world. I was designed to contract, to gather my energy, so that I could step forward with more power to my elbow.

I was designed as a perfect being, able to ride the roller coaster waves of this amazing adventure, to live all the vagaries of this imperfect human existence and not have to be ashamed of it.

I was designed to live a strong and powerful life and not be relegated to a back seat, a hidden room, a hole in the ground.

I was designed to stand loud and proud, to be a beacon of

light and to serve my true purpose in the world.

I was designed to put myself out there, to take a hit for humanity and to bounce back, so that you can see that, if I was designed this way, then you were too.

9th May 2020

Not Ready

I'm waiting for Boris's announcement and truth be told I'm scared about what he might say. I don't want to move freely amongst other people's germs and risk life and limb just so I can have a beer with friends, or a meal out or watch the latest film.

Things that I used to love, scare the hell out of me now. I wouldn't mind if I could see the virus, you know, if it were some kind of flashing neon orb, floating around in the air that I could step around. But who knows what I'd be walking into.

I imagine the grey globules with dark red prickles, burrs that will attach themselves to my lungs with every inhale, invade every part of my body and attack my organs. Their steel-edged thorns ready to cut, dissect and rip me apart and leave me for dead.

I don't want to quit my house to mill around with a hundred other folk. I want to stay home in my safe haven, with my comfort blanket and my deep blue pacifier. I want to keep the world at bay, by at least two metres and know that no-one is going to breach my boundaries.

I want to sit in the garden, read my book, enjoy my downtime and work at a slow pace. I'm not ready to get back into the rat race. I don't want to rush headlong into my old life. I want time to think, to reflect and decide how I want my new normal to look, so that when I get my freedom back, I'm not running blind again.

10th May 2020

It is...

I didn't write a daily yarn today.
    I ran out of time.
    I could have a load of thinking about it.
    But it is what it is.

11th May 2020

War Zone

I watch the news and feel a groundswell of venomous rage. I sit on my sofa and rant and rave at the television.

The world is wrong. Journalists are asking the wrong questions. Politicians are saying the wrong things. People are taking the wrong action, making their own absurd choices, ignoring well intentioned advice. Everyone, except me of course, is caught up in the stupidity of their thinking, even the people who should be in control. Boy am I angry!

My heart contracts, my pulse races. Poison gushes from the nerve center, carried through my bloodstream and does untold damage. My body is under attack. An army of invisible terrorists bomb my equilibrium, guerillas stab at my internal defenses, militiamen hijack and crucify my sanity. My head feels like it is severed from my soul.

I'm in a war zone in my own front room.

What good does it do, to blame, judge and criticise from the comfort of my own lounge? It falls on deaf ears. My voice hangs in the air, only to drop, inert, like a stone to the ground.

What difference does it make, to the journalists, or the Government, or even the world, if I get angry here, where they can't see me? We all know the answer to that one.

But what happens if I choose not to fight with the TV screen?

The outside world would still be the same, but my world, the inner condition of my life, boy does that change! OMG the difference is huge! A ceasefire, a truce, an end to hostilities. The armies withdraw, the poison dissipates, my head reconnects and peace washes over me like a warm bath.

I can choose anger, or I can choose peace and for my own sake, I choose peace.

12th May 2020

Writing Yarns

These daily yarns are a bit of a mystery to me. I think that I am an instrument and the words come from a place other than me. I mean sometimes my head tries to have a say, but that often gets edited out.

It astounds me how every day I can write about new and different subjects. Let me tell you, sometimes I write words that I don't even know what they mean and when I look them up later, they are just perfect. How does that happen? I once used the word 'ubiquitous'. Great word isn't it! I had no idea what it meant and when I looked it up, you could have knocked me down with a feather, I couldn't have chosen a better word.

Every day, new daily yarns appear on the page and it's a mystery to me where they come from.

I don't plan what I'm going to write about, and that's the truth. I've just given the game away right there, let the cat out of the bag, told you how I pull the rabbit out of the hat. That's half the secret behind this magic trick. There's no mystery, it's plain as day. Sit down, with a pen in my hand, with nothing on my mind. My only plan is to use Jack Grapes Method Writing. That's the other half of the secret.

Sometimes the pen whizzes across the page and I can barely keep up, sometimes it's slow and languorous and it takes it's time, and then again sometimes it's like pulling teeth.

The first piece of writing is the story making itself known to me – I think it was Terry Pratchett that said that, not me. But I know what he means. The story comes through me and then my job, the real work is to edit it into shape.

13th May 2020

Dog Tired

I went to bed very early last night. I couldn't wait to snuggle into the fresh comforting embrace of cotton sheets and feather pillows. I was so dog tired.

The kind of tired when my head feels like a ten pound bowling ball, when the strings to my mouth won't work, and the words slop out onto the table, when I don't have the energy to eat my beloved chocolate, my most favourite ritual of the day.

The hours I've been working have been stacking up, but everything felt so different that I didn't notice. I'm doing zoom calls, instead of face to face meetings, so I had time to do more of them. I'm attending more webinars, offering more free services, writing more, walking more, cycling more, eating at home more, preparing food and washing up more, cleaning the house more.

Plus… I'm carrying the pandemic like a weighted cloak around my shoulders.

I've been behaving as if I'm some cartoon superhero, but those powers are a figment of my imagination.

I've been trying to make everything seem normal, but we're not in normal times, and trying to be normal has taken too much out of me.

Last night the herculean effort caught up with me.

Yesterday I dragged myself through three online meetings, forced myself to write, then sent some emails before I caved in to the overwhelming exhaustion and ground to a massive full stop.

I was in bed by nine o'clock and asleep before my head hit the pillow. I slept the sleep of the dead, as my old dad used to say, and I didn't wake up till the alarm went off at 7.30am.

The weight on my shoulders has not disappeared, the cloak of the pandemic is hard to shrug off, but the bowling ball doesn't weigh quite so much today.

14th May 2020

Family Bond

I'm looking forward to seeing my sister today, even if it is two metres apart. It will be good to see more than just her head and shoulders, without her fading in and out, rebuffering, and to hear whole sentences all in one go!

We're going to drive to a beautiful local location in our separate cars and take a walk at a socially acceptable distance. The last time we took a walk together was so long ago. Well before lockdown. In the grist of life, we'd somehow forgotten the simple pleasure of spending a few hours together taking a walk, just for the sake of it.

I've got a lump in my throat at the thought. My heart is swollen, awash with love and my eyes fill with watery emotion when I think about seeing her this afternoon. It's been a long time since I appreciated any member of my family as much as I do today.

With our family, sometimes we see each other often and then other times it might be months before we get together again. That's our normal. We know we love each other. In times of trouble it's a cast iron guarantee that we're there to provide support, but we don't need to live in each other's pockets. There's a love that holds us together that time and distance can never break.

Today I am reminded of that bond. Today I don't take them

for granted. Today I remember the depth of my love for my family and maybe tomorrow I'll take them for granted again but that's OK too.

15th May 2020

Another Day

Another day to breathe
   To wax lyrical about life's treasures
   To dig deep into my heart
   And see what I can find there
   To draw from the well of human elixir
   To float in the space
   Between stars
   To be buoyed up
   By life's cushioned waters
   To relax, let go and surrender
   To what is
   And what will be

Another day to see
   The extraordinary
   Ordinariness
   Of a trillion million miracles
   To coin a previous phrase
   To step by slow and grateful step
   To spin and
   Yet not spin
   To be pulled down and
   Yet not be pulled

To walk and
Yet not move forward
To stop and
Yet not remain

Another day to cook
To clean and to keep house
To brush the dust away from
Previous days
To watch TV
To say hello and have a cup of tea
To make a phone call
To have a chat
To relish this
Ordinary existence

16th May 2020

Happy Monday

I hope you had a great weekend.
   I hope you rested well.
   I hope you had fun and laughter and joy ever after.

I hope you come to Monday with a lightness of spirit,
   full of the joys of Spring,
   with a happy heart.

I hope you come to Monday
   knowing how precious a Monday can be,
   the same as every other day of the week.

I hope you come to Monday
   knowing how precious you are.

I hope you come to Monday
   knowing how precious life is
   and don't fritter part of it away by hating Mondays.

18th May 2020

Supermarket Fear

I went to the supermarket for the first time in six weeks. It didn't look so different. The car park and the store looked the same. The makeshift garden centre outside, filled with plants, trees, flowerpots and compost, that wasn't there before, but that's not so unusual.

The black and yellow taped lines on the ground, the orange barricades and the black arrows, they were new. Being herded into a one way system, that was new. The girl in the high vis vest, she was new too.

The trolleys were stacked in their usual place. There was no one sanitising the handles. I had to believe that someone had done that already, that was hard. Did I trust, or should I just go home?

I pushed on and took a trolley after putting on my home-made mask. That was unusual too. I thought everyone would be wearing one, but it was only me. Am I the only one too scared to venture out without a shield?

People pushed past me, reached around me, got too close for comfort. Am I the only one keeping a social distance?

As I pushed the trolley towards the car, I noticed my heart pounding and the adrenaline pumping around my body like I've just run a one horse race. I took the cotton veil from my face and let go of the breath that I didn't even know I was holding. I drove home, grateful that I didn't have to run this gauntlet again until next week.

Am I the only one who feels this afraid?

19th May 2020

In My Mind

In my mind I can fly to exotic places, cold or hot, dry deserts or tropical gardens, relax by a pool with a good book or take a hike up Kilimanjaro, which would probably kill me if I did it for real.

In my mind I can choose my destination and the route by which I travel. I can choose to be adventurous and take risks, swim through shark filled waters or trundle through mosquito infested jungles or ride roughshod down extreme mountain tracks, with a thousand foot drop by the side of me, sweating with fear and trepidation, but still enjoy the ride.

In my mind I can look at calm waters, sit on a quiet beach and stare out at the vast expanse of a millpond ocean, enjoy the warm sun on my back and sit in awe and wonder at the majesty of life.

In my mind I can choose my experience. I can choose a lockdown prison or a safe haven, fear of the unknown or rest in the fact of now. I can choose bewilderment, confusion and turmoil or peace, quiet and stillness, a tranquility that resides beyond the excruciating noise that sometimes occupies my mind.

I can ride all the waves, no matter how extreme, accommodate all the roller coaster drops, into what sometimes looks oblivion, and experience every nuance of this human life, knowing that in my mind I can choose my response to any of it.

20th May 2020

Birthday Reflection

I have another birthday coming up. Another year has flown by. I'm another step closer to the departure lounge and what do I have to show for it?

I could write you a list of all my achievements but what are they now? Just memories, sandcastles washed away by the sea, moments in time that I thought meant something.

I could show you my CV, but what would it really tell you about me. I'm not my list of job descriptions, my qualifications, not even my hobbies.

I could tell you about my good deeds, my donations to charity, my random acts of kindness but what are they to you if you were not on the receiving end and did not see them.

I'm not the one who can see what I have to show for my life, it's you who will write my epitaph. It's how I showed up that will be remembered.

21st May 2020

Human Kindness

I can believe that I make no difference in the world, that I am insignificant, that my actions are meaningless, that I'm not big enough, famous enough or rich enough to make a mark on the planet.

I can question, till the cows come home, my purpose on this earth, draw a blank and withdraw into my little self.

I can join in the rank and file, with the followers of fashion, keep my own views and thoughts to myself and not stick my head above the parapet.

I can scare myself into submission and rely on someone else to lead the way. Someone who is stronger, more confident, more self-assured than me. Someone who will stand up for what I know is true in my heart of hearts, that human kindness is the way forward.

I can tell myself that my own small acts of human kindness, my soft spoken words and my own peace and calm are but tiny raindrops on the ocean.

But where would the ocean be, without the rain?

22nd May 2020

23rd May 2020

Dominic Cummings, Boris Johnson's chief political adviser, comes under mounting pressure to resign after it was revealed that he travelled 260 miles from London to Durham to self-isolate during lockdown and while his wife was displaying COVID-19 symptoms.

(I mention this only because it dominated the news for several days and the effect of the onslaught can be seen in later daily yarns!)

Headline News

A woman in Leicestershire, unknown to 99.999% of the population, received a million and one blessings on her birthday.

She is reported as saying "I never knew there was so much love and kindness in the world."

If you passed her in the street, you wouldn't give her a second glance, she's as ordinary a woman as you would ever meet.

So why does this shy, reserved individual warrant such a shower of tender generosity and unexpected benevolence?

"I really have no idea." She said in response to this inquisitive questioner.

"Perhaps it's that people see themselves in me, they see their own humanity and it's easier to show love to another person than it is to love themselves." She said.

"My dearest wish is that one day they will see this love and know that when they give it away to others they receive it too."

25th May 2020

25th May 2020

George Floyd, a black American man, was killed today while being arrested in Minneapolis.
A witness recorded it happening and millions saw the video as it circulated the globe via social media.

(Although this news is not related to COVID-19, it had a significant impact on me (and millions of others) and is reflected in some of the daily yarns that follow.)

Kevlar

Why do I keep thinking it's February? Do I yearn for a safer time and place?

A time when fear was not so much a daily feature as an errant whimsy that would raise its head every so often.

When fear was 'in your face obvious', before it hurtled into my life and trampled on my existence.

When fear was not an undercurrent that permeates every moment, a silent scream that runs below the surface and without a blaze of glory, adds a dose of poison. Not enough to kill, but enough to leave a foul taste in my mouth, like milk that's a day over.

How do I let go of fear that is less like a hot coal and more like a thorned rose stem? Succulent leaves form a cushion, but don't quite block the needle sharp pricks. The pain is uncomfortable yet bearable. If I let go of the stem, I risk the loss of the bloom.

Fear taints the aroma and blinds my eye to its full beauty. I see life through a gossamer veil and it's made of Kevlar.

This fear thinks it's protective, a shield to ward off dangerous spirits. What if it is?

In the heat of the sun, I resent the weight of it, it feels like too warm a coat, yet if I was in a full-on collision, I'd be grateful that I wore it. I judge that it hides under the surface, rather than be grateful that it doesn't overwhelm me.

I forget that I put it on and take it off, like a change of clothes, when I choose what's appropriate for the weather.

When storms appear in my mind, I don my Kevlar. It protects me from the worst of it. In the lining of my consciousness, it saves me from far worse consequences.

26th May 2020

My Prayer

My cage has been rattled, shaken and stirred. The pot is molten, the ground is no longer sure, the volcano has erupted, the earth has quaked in its boots, the ash has not yet settled and the air is thick with doom.

The world is a hell hole of hate, anger and blame. Love and understanding be damned. Kindness forgotten. Gratitude is a dirty word.

It turned on a sixpence, this U-turn back to darker days.

It had seemed that a new order was on its way, but maybe it was too scary, too foreign, too much of the unknown, too quick. Unaccustomed as we'd become to our true selves, we've reverted to type.

The world has donned a familiar pair of, what used to be comfortable, old boots. But our feet have grown, along with our hearts, and now the boots are the wrong size and shape and cramp our true nature.

I hope and pray that we will see that the old way doesn't fit any more, that love and understanding will return and the world will be a more comfortable place.

27th May 2020

The News Effect

I've stopped watching the news, listening to the news, reading the news, talking about the news. I hate what it does to me. My head feels like it will explode, my heart pounds into a rage and a red mist clouds my eyes.

I'm Boadicea on her war ready chariot, with my shield and spear in the air, ready to fight to the death for a return to common sense and balance.

I know it's an inside-out world, but Oh my God, it sure doesn't look that way when I get into this state. It looks a lot to me like the players on the TV, the words on the page, the roar from the journalist's mouths is what causes my disturbance.

I know it's not an outside-in world, but sometimes it's hard to see where the outside ends and the inside starts.

I know it's not true that '**they**' are the creators of my experience, but when I'm in this state of mind, the best I can do is switch the television off and wait for my peace of mind to return because otherwise, the price I pay is my equilibrium.

28th May 2020

Wish me Luck

The date is getting close, when the competition result is announced and the fate of my book will be decided.

I tell myself not to get my hopes up, not to bank on the outcome, not to bet on being the winner. The odds are too small. But no matter, I've already spent the prize money!

I'm an optimist by nature and failure is not on my radar. No matter there's a hundred of us and only one can win. "We're all winners in this race." Says the snide voice in the back of my mind, that doesn't know any better.

I've worked hard on this, put all my eggs in this basket. No matter that my chances are slim, someone has to win and why shouldn't it be me. I ignore the tinny voice that says why would it be and pretend the other writers don't exist.

I've done well not to think about it, but as the deadline approaches, it plays on my mind. Maybe the decision has been made, maybe the winner already knows, maybe it's not me after all. Every day without a word is a step closer to doom.

I tell myself a thousand times that it won't be the end of the world if I don't win, that it's not the winning it's the taking part, that there's always a plan B. It's cold comfort.

It's only a few more days. I don't know if I can bear it, not that I have a choice. Think of me here at home, as I bite my

tongue and wait for my fate.
   Please wish me luck.

29th May 2020

Author's note: The competition was won by another writer.
I've now reverted to plan B.

1st June 2020

The easing of lockdown restrictions began today.

Good Student

I'm a Grade A pupil. I do the exercise like I was taught. I'm the first to put my hand up, the first to answer the question, the first to turn in my homework.

I ignore the hatred of other students. They think I'm teacher's pet, but not even he likes me, this smart Alec know it all, who thinks she's better than the rest of us.

I ignore the groans and the venom that spits in my direction, from all corners of the classroom, when my hand shoots into the air.

I ignore the grudge in the A Plus mark, the pinch in the commendation, the only half disguised pleasure when I get it wrong.

I push on with the thought that, if I do well in class, I will get my reward.

I hold myself up as a good student, hold myself up to be shot down, hold myself to ransom with the idea that I should know the answers, I should be an expert, I should be perfect, because if I'm not then what am I?

I'm a failure, a has been, a two-bit hoe.

I crucify myself with the notion that the world thinks I should be better, when all it asks is that I be me.

1st June 2020

Complicit Contribution

All my life I've seen bad things happen, through the lens of the television and media. It's always been far away and not within my sphere of influence. Being the good person that I am, I hoped and prayed for a better world. I thought that if I just be nice, that would be enough to make a difference.

A recent conversation opened my eyes a fraction. From my fully able, straight, white perspective I had not seen the condescension in well-meaning language, and the inherent haughtiness in Society's day to day treatment of people who are different. I put the blame at Society's door, with no acknowledgement that I am part of Society.

Then George Floyd was murdered in America and in amongst my horror, I was grateful that we don't have that problem here in the UK. I'm so tempted to erase that sentence, to deny my ignorance, to pretend that I didn't really think that. The truth is, I know that we have our own versions of it over here, but in my safe home, I wear blinkers. I choose to see only the good in the world.

My eyes are being opened to my own complicity in a world of prejudice and hate. My inaction, however good my intentions, has done nothing to improve the situation.

I don't know yet what to do but I know that I'm being called. I don't know enough about the problem to bring about change and that's a good place for me to start. I don't know what the answer is yet, but I know it's based in love.

I'll start with owning my own complicit contribution and choose, with love in my heart, to see, to take my blinkers off, to take note and from a place of wisdom, take action.

2nd June 2020

Rebellion's End

After last week's little rebellion, I realise now that I do have to watch the News.

How else do I find out what's happening in the world?

How else do I hear about prejudice and injustice?

How else will I know what I have to stand for or against?

All these years I've been selective about what I pay attention to. I've lived in my own cosy bubble where I've been closeted and protected from ugliness in the world. I've been able to pretend it doesn't exist and go about my daily life unharmed, yet ignorant.

I knew that bad stuff happened, but it wasn't in my backyard, so apart from throwing my hands up in horror, I did nothing.

Events this week have woken me up to the fact that the world will not be a better place unless people act. Up till now I've relied on other people, ignoring the fact that I'm 'people' too.

First things first, I need to educate myself. I need to know what's happening, and why, before I can know what I need to do. There are ways and means to do that and one of those is to watch the News.

I know I'm going to get aerated when I do. As I said last week, it upsets my peace of mind. But what's a little disturbance to my equilibrium, compared to what some people are going through in the world. And, when I get disturbed, that's how I know that there's something to stand up for.

3rd June 2020

Only Love

Right now, I don't know what to do. I don't know what to say. I don't know the next course of action. And when I don't know, I get nervous and anxious, like I should know.

I forget that wisdom is my guide and that an inner voice is letting me know what to do, even when I think I don't know.

When I reflect back on the last few days I see how wisdom guided me back to watch the news, to speak to my mentor, to order a particular book, to talk to people about what's happening, and to share my experience of being woken up, to the part I need to play in world events.

When I was caught up in horror, shame and guilt, the quiet voice of wisdom still moved me in the right direction. It brought to mind Martin Luther King, Ghandi and Nelson Mandela, all proponents of love in the face of racism, prejudice and hate. Wisdom guided me to look at what was happening from a place of love.

I had this idea that wise action in the face of widespread ugliness, should be big and dramatic and have a massive impact, when in fact, small steps, often taken, coming from love, take us in the right direction and this is wisdom in action.

I see thousands of people doing the same thing, taking small steps from a place of love. When I count them, they add up to a huge wave of love making its way around the world. It gives me hope and comfort to keep on doing what I'm doing, because I know that, although I am but a small droplet, I am an integral part of that ocean of love that will make a difference in the world.

So I remain guided my Martin Luther King who said;
"Hate cannot drive out hate, only love can do that."

4th June 2020

5th June 2020

The number of UK recorded deaths from COVID-19 exceeded 40,000.

People in the UK started to protest for Black Lives Matter following in the footsteps of thousands of others in the USA.

Force for Good

Here's some of my flaws:

I rant and rave in my own front room, but I do nothing.

I've never written to my local Member of Parliament.

Sometimes I've not voted.

Sometimes I've voted without knowing who or what I'm voting for.

I buy online because it's easier than going to my local store.

I send plastic to landfill when I don't want to wash it out.

I buy plastic packaged goods because it's convenient.

I don't often buy ethically sourced clothes.

I jump in the car, when it would take ten minutes on my bike.

I've been silent on many issues.

I've been ashamed of these imperfections, but not enough to do anything about them.

I've papered over the cracks of my own human frailties. I've hidden in my wholeness so that I don't have to look at the dark side of my soul. I've turned away from my shortcomings, kept them locked away in the closet, out of the sight of others.

It's not that I think I'm any different to anyone else, I know that's not true.

I'm not looking for you to tell me that I'm not a bad

person, I know that already. I know I'm not on my own. I know it's not just me, but that doesn't make it right.

Recent events have opened my eyes to my contribution to the global condition, whether it's climate change, racism, plastic waste, poverty, inequality or any one of the myriad issues that the world faces.

As I take a long hard look at my frailties I can see where my responsibility lies and I know what I need to do so that I am a force for good for both humanity and the planet.

5th June 2020

Dreaded Association

I had quite the dream last night. It was very ordinary, yet the feeling was like the magnetic pull of gravity and it sucked me down into a vice like jaw. The jeopardy was palpable, and though my eyes could not see the source, I knew my life was in mortal danger.

When I woke up, I tried to fix the dream, as I so often do when I wake from a nightmare, but the dream was adamant in its account and nothing I did altered the feeling.

I couldn't marry the content of the story to the fear that threatened to overwhelm me. It was like there was a veil over my eyes that stopped me from seeing.

I drifted between nightmare and wakeful state and did my best to rouse myself each time the horror took hold. I told myself there was nothing to be scared of, it was only a dream, yet the nightmare continued.

Later as I sat in the garden with the warm sun on my face and in the quiet of a Sunday morning, the name of the veil popped into my mind.

I saw how I have worn this veil for many years, and most especially through these last few weeks.

I saw how scared I get about ordinary matters and stories that I make up in my mind.

I saw how it's not the story that creates my fear, but my

response to it and the meaning I associate it with.

I saw the name of the veil and it made perfect sense. The name of the veil is Dread.

8th June 2020

Time for Bed

I'm wondering if there's a daily yarn left in me or whether it is time to stop. The pandemic isn't over, but lockdown is easing and maybe it's time to ease into something new.

This curious time has brought out a roller coaster ride of emotion in me and it's been interesting to ride the waves.

There was a time when I thought that many of my feelings meant that there was something wrong with me. In fact, I spent much of my adult life in pursuit of an answer to the question "What's wrong with me and how do I fix it?"

I believed that underneath this glossy exterior there was a flawed human being. I tried everything. I tried to work out what the flaws were, where they came from, how they started. I tried to gloss over them with positive affirmations. I tried to change my thinking, ignore my thinking, pretend my thinking did not exist. I tried to put my best foot forward but what's the point of that when you know your best is not good enough.

I dug myself into a hole in the search. The longer I delved into it, the bigger it got and the deeper I got cemented into the idea that there was something wrong with me.

In all those years I never questioned the question. I never challenged the assumption that I was flawed. I never asked where that idea came from. I never saw that, the fact that I could weather all these different emotions, pointed to the simple but profound truth that I was already whole.

It's been a fun ride, mining the depth and breadth of this lockdown experience, in the interest of creative writing. I've enjoyed sharing the ride with you.

It's not the end of my creative writing and I will continue to share. But I think it's time to put my daily yarns to bed.

9th June 2020

About me&dee Charity

Some of the proceeds from every sale of this book will be donated to me&dee Charity.

This is a wonderful little charity with a massive heart. It is based in Derbyshire and provides holidays to families, from all over the UK, facing life changing or life limiting circumstances. For the families, life can be an endless round of hospitals, treatments and surgeries and the holidays give them some respite from that, but more important is the opportunity to make special memories, that the surviving members can hold onto for the rest of their lives.

It's a charity that does not tick the usual boxes in order to access funding, so everything they do relies on the donations of many people on a regular basis. It costs over £400 per person per holiday, and they aim to help around 100 families a year, so you can see that they need every penny.

The story of how this charity came into existence is a story worth reading in itself. Please check out their website www.meanddee.co.uk, to read Maria Hanson MBE's story of how the charity came about, find out more about their work, and perhaps make a donation.

About the Author

Maria Iliffe-Wood is the author of Coaching Presence, Building Consciousness and Awareness into Coaching Interventions. She works with leaders, coaches and writers to help them to see a deeper wisdom that resides within each and every one of us.

She has been a voracious reader her whole life, but never saw herself as a writer, nor as an academic, which just goes to prove that you can't believe everything you think.

She lives in Leicestershire in the UK, with her husband Ash.

To find out more about Maria's work go to www.fromquiet.co.uk, and for more about her writing, check out www.iliffe-wood.co.uk. You can follow her on Facebook or Instagram @iliffewood or connect with her on Linked In.

Gratitude

For a little book there are quite a few people without whom it would not exist, but I don't have the room to list each and every one of you, so if you don't see your name, please know that you are in here.

The first person to thank is always my husband Ash. Every morning he sits patient and quiet while I write. He never offers me anything but love and encouragement. I cannot put into words how much of a difference that makes to me, not just in my writing but in my life.

Second has got to be my writing coach and mentor Jules Swales, without whom my writing would be entirely different. (And yes Jules I'll pay the $5 for that adverb). I am so grateful for all I have learned from her and continue to learn, she is the perfect mix of wise teacher and loving and supportive friend.

And I must mention the other two members of our little writing club - Jacqueline Hollows and Jamie Fiore-Higgins, who are a wonderful source of inspiration and encouragement.

Dicken Bettinger, thank you for your wonderful mentorship over so many years, and your gentle guidance in my exploration of how love and life works and Coizie Bettinger for being such a wonderful role model and for your most loving and ardent support of all my yarns. I cannot tell you how grateful I am, to call you both my friends.

Jan and Chip Chipman, we may not have seen you very often, but you have left a deep imprint on my soul.

Lucy Sheffield, thank you so much for your constant enthusiasm for my writing and your practical help in getting this book into existence.

Thank you to Karina Lyburn Photography for the back cover photo.

This is where the list gets too long to mention everyone else! I must also thank all of my friends and followers on Facebook and Instagram, for taking the time to read, comment and tell me how much of a difference the Daily Yarns made in your life during lockdown. I would never have continued writing them for so long without that.

From the bottom of my heart; THANK YOU.

Photo credits:

Back cover photo: Karina Lyburn Photography
Front cover photo canva.com Angie from Pexels

Printed in Great Britain
by Amazon

44318016R00111